MW01093468

"While many run
embraced this sil
biblical psalms th
intimacy with Go... ...— —————— ——— ——— collection of poems is
quite accurate—feeling the silence really does welcome wisdom
into the soul."

—PAUL B. MACKE, SJ
Jesuit Mission Coordinator, Jesuit Spiritual Center, Milford, Ohio

"Drawing on his personal and pastoral counseling experiences, Kohl
invites his readers through poetry and prayer to pay attention to
feelings, movements, vulnerabilities, and relational challenges that
can open a man's world to deeper intimacy . . . Spiritual seekers will
find prayer themes of healing of wounds, surrender, and relational
transformation in this book. Although *Feeling the Silence* is intended
for men and their intimacy needs, women may also benefit."

—FRAN REPKA, RSM
Spiritual Director

"These poems, and the prayers with them, come in dialogue with
other spiritual writers and Scripture. It makes for an absorbing
kind of book, full of surprises. Kohl takes risks on our behalf."

—RICHARD BOLLMAN, SJ
Retreat and Spiritual Ministry, Cincinnati, Ohio

"Chuck pours his very soul into these poems and then gifts them to
us. I am grateful! There's solid evidence here of 'God in all things' for
those who might doubt that, especially men who may not know how
to be vulnerable to the Spirit. There's deep wisdom here as well, but
be forewarned: this journey isn't with a pabulum Jesus. There's grit
here, with lots of struggle, surrender, and hard-won insight through
one man's marvelously intimate friendship with God."

—SEAN P. REYNOLDS
Cofounder, Mustard Seed Consultants

"In his quest for intimacy with the God of love, Chuck has used spiritual writings of others he calls 'launchings' to guide him more deeply into prayer and into God. Here he provides fresh and sensual poetry to 'nudge' and 'launch' you men who are also seekers. Let these writings move you toward and into the God of love, who is eager to welcome you."

—JANE CASSERLY MYERS
Director of Parish Life, Bellarmine Chapel, Xavier University

Feeling The Silence

Feeling The Silence

Welcoming Wisdom into the Male Soul

CHARLES A. KOHL

RESOURCE *Publications* • Eugene, Oregon

FEELING THE SILENCE
Welcoming Wisdom Into the Male Soul

Resource Publications
An Imprint of Wipf and Stock Publishers
199 W. 8th Ave., Suite 3
Eugene, OR 97401

www.wipfandstock.com

PAPERBACK ISBN: 978-1-6667-0607-9
HARDCOVER ISBN: 978-1-6667-0608-6
EBOOK ISBN: 978-1-6667-0609-3

09/20/21

This book is dedicated to:
My wife, Kathy, for your openness to being the primary
conduit of the Holy Spirit's work on my heart.

My children Ashley, Rachel, Sarah, and Joey for your patience
with me as I learned to be a father.

Mike Myers for once, several years ago, asking "When are you
going to write a book?"

Beginning

WHILE LINGERING ON A precipice at the South Kaibab Trailhead in The Grand Canyon, I first realized the tangibility and authenticity of my prayer. A silence emanating from the depth of earth pulsated, pressed upon me, and invited me deeper. My wife Kathy's thumb and forefinger gripping my loose shirt kept me grounded—if not for her, I might have surrendered to the enticing lure of the experience's sense of depth and reality.

I'm certain some meteorologists can express in barometric terms why the lovely pressure of that silence fell upon me and intoxicated me on that glorious spring morning. The scientists' explanations are correct. I trust in their evidence. Yet, I'm equally confident many of those educated people could not convey why God used those barometric and atmospheric truths to not only speak to me but also, to assure me our relationship is real, palpable, and inebriating.

In this small book, I offer a glimpse into one man's sitting with God in that same silence that enveloped me at the head of the South Kaibab Trail. What you will read comes from my initial response to what many have called a mid-life crisis. For you who teeter on the edge or have just transitioned through a mid-life crisis, I hope my example will offer a more healing response than a fancy new car or new, superficial relationships.

I intend to encourage men to be open to God's call toward intimacy. I don't discount or wish to neglect that same call women experience in their relationship with God. Men in our society need more encouragement to be open and vulnerable to God and to understand that God desires relationship with them.

Typically, our society does not give men permission to be open to God's movement. I hope these examples of my prayers, in poetic form, offer a pathway for others to experience God as I have. Further, as I write this introduction, I wonder if what I offer are not so much poems as they are my psalms; odes giving witness to our living God's work in my life and my observation of the same in the lives of others.

I am just a regular guy. I'm not a theologian or scripture scholar. I've worked in corporate America my adult life and have had all the struggles and joys that come with thirty-two years of marriage, four beautiful children, and (so far) three jewels of my heart, my grandchildren. I'm like many who have turned to prayer as a response to crisis. The only difference is that I get to tell my story and expose my vulnerability to you—almost as if called by God to do so. This is my privilege that I want to share with you.

My consistent practice of engaging in prayer has been through spiritual writings or scripture, which I've heard described as "launching pads." In the same silence found at South Kaibab Trailhead and with a good spiritual director's help, I have sat in silence with God (believe me, it takes a great deal of patience). And after, I have journaled to capture what I experienced in that silence.

With the help of my skillful copy editor, I have taken my scribblings from my prayer journals and translated them into poetry. Assigned to each poem is the date the experience was recorded in my prayer journal. Along with each poem, with only a few exceptions, you'll see an excerpt of the spiritual writing or scripture I used to "launch."

If any words in this book appeal to you, and you choose to respond to a crisis, stressor, or joy in your life by turning to prayer, I strongly encourage you to seek the assistance of a professional spiritual director. To find a spiritual director ask your pastor, if you have one, or connect with Spiritual Directors International at https://www.sdicompanions.org/. Last, if you decide to engage with God in this or any similar way, I encourage patience. Be gentle with yourself. Avoid undue self-inflicted pressure to "accomplish" something. Let God do God's work.

God be with you.

What I say to you in the darkness, speak in the light;
what you hear whispered, proclaim on the housetops.

—MATTHEW 10:27

Acknowledgments

I COULD NOT HAVE come to relationship with God without the help of many beloved people in my life. By encouraging my continued willingness to surrender to God's desire to be in relationship, these people have helped me more than I can say. Among those, my wife Kathy has been the primary conduit of the Holy Spirit's work in softening my heart. Kathy's patience, forgiveness, and steadfast faithfulness have given me a glimpse, every day, into what the love and mercy of God are like. When I wake up, if she's still lying in bed next to me, I thank God she has not come to her senses.

Spiritual direction and formation are important in exploring and unpacking our prayer experiences. I thank my first spiritual director, the late Fr. Tom Ryan, S.J., for gently helping me explore this sacred silence and leading me to wade deeper with each new experience of God. Subsequently, Fr. Jim Schutte, my current spiritual director, deserves recognition for walking with me as I learn to name and tame the demons attempting to divert my attention from my relationship with God.

My parish's Director of Formation and Pastoral Care, Jane Myers, recognized early in my transition the Holy Spirit's work on my heart. As that work continued and deepened, Jane invited me to participate more fully in ministry—the training and development opportunities aimed toward companioning others' efforts in their exploration of their relationship with God. Jane helped me see how God wants to be in relationship with each of us in a unique way, and she continues that support to this day. Along with

Acknowledgments

Jane, I thank former pastors who created the space in our faith community where Ignatian Spirituality (www.ignatianspirituality.com) can be pursued as a primary means to understand and recognize God's movement and presence in our lives and our community. Those influential pastors are Fr. Richard Bollman, S.J., Fr. Dan Hartnett, S.J., and Fr. Tom Lawler, S.J.

Along those same lines of embracing Ignatian Spirituality, I thank Fr. Paul Macke, S.J., Sr. Fran Repka, R.S.M. for creating and inviting me to participate in a Spiritual Direction Internship Program. I've had the opportunity to continue exploring my relationship with God by walking with others as they explore their relationship with God.

I particularly thank Sean and Leah Reynolds for their deep friendship and love, for letting me be their servant when they needed it most, and for being our servants when we needed them. Connected with these two good friends, Mary Anne Reese deserves thanks for her continued encouragement, feedback, and support as I engaged in this writing and publication process.

A good support system is crucial for us to grow together in faith. The men of my small faith community we call Whiskey, Wings, and Wisdom have supported and reinforced the necessity for all of us to be vulnerable before God and each other. This is a means to allow God to continue pouring God's grace into our hearts. Those men are Dan Aerni, Jeff Borden, Phil Borden, Tom Green, Russ Martin, Chris (Curly) Shea, Greg Schloemer, Mark Stockman, and others.

My Copy Editor Robbi Sommers Bryant deserves recognition for her patient care in guiding the refinement of this process to transition feelings into words.

Finally, I want to acknowledge my sister-in-law, Michele Snyder, for her courage and her witness. Shortly after much of the prayer experience depicted in this book began, and not knowing about my new prayer practices, she revealed to me that I had found great favor with the Lord, Jesus.

June 7, 2012

"In the interior life there should be moments of relaxation, freedom and 'browsing.' Perhaps the best way to do this is in the midst of nature, but also in literature. Perhaps also a certain amount of art is necessary, and music . . . You also need a good garden, and you need access to the woods, or to the sea. Get out in those hills and really be in the midst of nature a little bit! That is not only legitimate, it is in a certain way necessary . . . The woods and nature should be part of your solitude, and if it's not periodically part of your solitude I think the law should be changed."

—Thomas Merton[1]

I trek the dark path to my soul
surrounded by bent trees, branches reaching.
Autumn leaves, forced from their security,
crunch under my feet
as the trail winds and wends to the ridge.
The moon, Your lantern, lights my way.

Moonlight and trees dance rhythmically
as light and dark collide
then bounce off each other like echoes,
confusing my senses.
The elements, too, seem perplexed.
But I am at peace.

1. Fox, Christian Mystics, day 301

The view from the top of my wooded soul clears,
offering me passage into some depth of my being.
Your love's burning fire allows me to bask
in the radiance that beckons me even deeper.

Your flames rise, narrow and tall,
to lick the stubborn walls of rock and earth
that stand against it.
Your tender touch invites the deeper cold
to open and be warmed.

Near Your fire,
I feel the burn yet remain unscathed.
Like You, I am patient,
as we wait
for the wall
to surrender.

June 30, 2012

"And in this purgation the devil flees away, for he has power over the soul only when it is attached to things corporeal and temporal"

—St. John of the Cross[1]

You give voice to Your love, filling my soul with gratitude.
You gaze upon me—
Your handiwork in me
and the bike I ride on this warm summer evening.
You touch it.
You test it.
You hold it just as I would.
And You speak to me.
Your word burrows to the depth of who I am.
Your word affirms my action,
my existence,
and Your will.
Your word enrages the angel
who desires to be the end of me.

---

1. Peers, John of the Cross, Ascent of Mount Carmel, 72

July 10, 2012

"Jesus was more human than humanity. His was the most human face of all. This is going to open up wonders for you."[1]

Humanity gathers around the old oak table.
The room, littered with documents and trinkets of a hoarder's life,
surrounds the game we play for joyous times.
The game anticipates our engagement,
dim light revealing only players' silhouettes—silver surrounding
black.

The unheard yet felt Voice invites us into roles.
The rules, rejected or embraced,
are written on our hearts.
Competing sounds of elation and fury
erupt from the truth we are or pretend to be.

From a corner shadow,
a serpent slithers eagerly toward
the intoxicating scent of opportunity.
Craving the anger, the culprit comes to tempt.
Pleasing the serpent is the ploy—
following blind complacency,
and the path of least resistance,
hoping to score more false security and love.

1. Eldridge, Beautiful Outlaw, 55

Attentive to the game of fate,
I avoid temptation's seduction.
Patiently, I wait my turn—
joyfully engaging with the players
while suffering the sting of their wrath.

July 20, 2012

"... it does not seem to me a waste of time if I go into it farther and offer you some consolation about it; though this will be of little help to you until the Lord is pleased to give us light. But it is necessary (and His Majesty's will) that we should take proper measures and learn to understand ourselves, and not blame our souls for what is the work of our weak imagination and our nature and the devil."

—St Theresa of Avila[1]

In this dark place, I sit calmly,
hoping You'll come.
This darkness soothes me,
demands nothing of me.
Its welcome envelope secures me in this peace,
where rest is made perfect,
and Your light is most easily seen.

You come to me.
Your presence slowly engages my vision
as a white point of light
revealing horizon and terrain to explore.

1. Peers, Teresa of Avila, Interior Castle, 61

Your light grows; invades my very being—
carries me in the swift current of Your love.
Your light drenches my heart in waves;
the tides pull me under and over themselves.

The pervasive light is alive—
hurls me forward in my surrender.
River of living light carries,
then dumps me into a gutter
where Your Ark,
ancient, wooden, abandoned,
waits for its footmen to carry it forward.

July 28, 2012

"For the desires that are living in the soul, so that it can-
not understand Him, will be swallowed by God by means
of chastisement and correction, either in this life or in the
next, and this will come to pass through purgation."[1]

Like a ghost, I stand in the doorway,
where the people of God
encircle the shell of a man
who lies breathless,
hoping to be left alone.

The monitors,
the pumps,
the caregivers
have stopped.
The man has stopped . . .

People of God cry.
Unchoreographed tears dance
with reckless abandon.
Happy tears expose the hearts
of these people of God.
I long to dance with these people of God,
present in this beauty,
where finitude intersects eternity.

1. Peers, John of the Cross, Ascent of Mount Carmel, 92

September 19, 2012

Then to what shall I compare the people of this generation? What are they like? They are like children who sit in the marketplace and call to one another, "'We played the flute for you, but you did not dance. We sang a dirge, but you did not weep." For John the Baptist came neither eating food nor drinking wine, and you said, "He is possessed by a demon." The Son of Man came eating and drinking and you said, "Look, he is a glutton and a drunkard, a friend of tax collectors and sinners." But wisdom is vindicated by all her children.

—LUKE 7:31–35

Wisdom's children
dine with tax collectors and pharisees.
Accompany the suffering a mile longer.
Welcome the outcasts to the table,
dance with the lame
patiently awaiting an invitation to the storm.

Pounding rain ravages the earth,
disguising all life with darkness and desolation.
Wisdom's children see through the façade,
repel the Emperor rising from the sea.

The Lover of Lies rises
in defiance of Wisdom's children.
The malevolent maestro spins the clouds into a violent maelstrom,
churning his watery abode into a battering ram.

Wisdom's children cry to the Lord, "Save us!"

September 20, 2012

(This event happened during my hour of Eucharistic Adoration at Our Lady of The Holy Spirit Center.)

> Now there was a sinful woman in the city who learned that he was at table in the house of the Pharisee. Bringing an alabaster flask of ointment, she stood behind him at his feet weeping and began to bathe his feet with her tears. Then she wiped them with her hair, kissed them, and anointed them with the ointment.
>
> —Luke 7:37–38

Next to me, a broken woman kneels,
spewing the depth of her sorrow and her pain.

Your grace draws her to You.
Your grace invites me to share
sacred space and time.

She weeps for her husband.
She weeps for her children.
She weeps for what she cannot see ahead of her.
Her tears fall at Your feet.
I sit in awe at your revelation of what will unfold next.

"¿Habla ingles?"
"No. Not good."
"God loves you, and I am sorry for your pain."
"My husband is in jail."

In a flash, the weeping woman leaves,
her trail of tears etched permanently into my soul.
You reveal a path carved by the woman's suffering,
leading me to the prison with my hand in Yours.

September 24, 2012

No one who lights a lamp conceals it with a vessel or sets it under a bed; rather, he places it on a lampstand so that those who enter may see the light. For there is nothing hidden that will not become visible, and nothing secret that will not be known and come to light. Take care, then, how you hear. To anyone who has, more will be given, and from the one who has not, even what he seems to have will be taken away.

—LUKE 8:16–18

Amid the din of contemporary voices,
and my life experience,
my ears hear Your call.
In my dualism,
I cry out for either/or.

My heart hears Your call
shrouded in the din of contemporary voices
and my life experience.
Adrenaline ignites a fire in my chest,
fueled by the hope
of being freed from the secular instruction manual, more awaits
me.

My ears hear Your call
beneath the din of contemporary voices
and my life experience.
Truth becomes unseen and unheard.
Hearing with only my ears,
I become blind to my neighbor.

My heart hears Your call
hidden in the din of contemporary voices
and my life experience.
The paradox of "both/and"
opening up becomes real,
becomes possible,
becomes liberating.

In "both/and," the truth is found and multiplied.
In letting go of myself, "both/and" is free
to weave itself like a tapestry
into my being,
where I find mystery and truth
in the golden fringes
where "either/or" cease to explain who You are.

September 26, 2012

He summoned the Twelve and gave them power and authority over all demons and to cure diseases, and he sent them to proclaim the kingdom of God and to heal [the sick]. He said to them, "Take nothing for the journey, neither walking stick, nor sack, nor food, nor money, and let no one take a second tunic. Whatever house you enter, stay there and leave from there. And as for those who do not welcome you, when you leave that town, shake the dust from your feet in testimony against them." Then they set out and went from village to village proclaiming the good news and curing diseases everywhere.

—LUKE 9:1–6

The demons lie in wait
for me to become tired,
hungry,
angry,
frustrated, distracted, and weak.

False hope of soothing their own isolation
fuels the demons' desire
to drag me down with them.
Hidden in my ego, like hungry ghosts,
they wait,
dressing themselves in fake hope and empty love.

Light hidden in my soul
yearns for freedom
to break through the fog,
to await my surrender—
the secret that drives the demons out.

Dishonest hope and deceitful love
masquerade as goodness.
But Your light burns away the vestments,
exposing the demons' true selves.

October 9, 2012

Therefore, it was necessary for the copies of the heavenly things to be purified by these rites, but the heavenly things themselves by better sacrifices than these. For Christ did not enter into a sanctuary made by hands, a copy of the true one, but heaven itself, that he might now appear before God on our behalf. Not that he might offer himself repeatedly, as the high priest enters each year into the sanctuary with blood that is not his own; if that were so, he would have had to suffer repeatedly from the foundation of the world. But now once for all he has appeared at the end of the ages to take away sin by his sacrifice. Just as it is appointed that human beings die once, and after this the judgment, so also Christ, offered once to take away the sins of many, will appear a second time, not to take away sin but to bring salvation to those who eagerly await him.

—HEB 9:23–28

Losing myself in the weight of the deep, dark firmament,
a silence builds upon itself until
it can no longer hold its joyful news.

Burnt light streaks from the horizon,
hinting at a special victory.

Blue, red, purple,
hundreds of points of light
spanning the spectrum follow,
rocketing slowly through my vision,
inciting celebration with pointillistic precision.

Points morph into clusters
radiating brilliance, goodness, softness, and excitement!
Clusters transform to flared silent horns.
Light reveals joy felt in those still trumpets.
Beautiful noise taps my sense regardless.

Sky alight with these comings and goings,
gathering, clumping, forming, heralding!

Heart and mind race with eagerness as my soul thirsts for more.
Excitement is left unfulfilled as the fiery trumpets
dissipate and transform
in my vision to the darkness.

Lead me to the trumpets!
It is not too late for either of us.

October 16, 2012

According to the grace of God given to me, like a wise master builder I laid a foundation, and another is building upon it. But each one must be careful how he builds upon it, for no one can lay a foundation other than the one that is there, namely, Jesus Christ. If anyone builds on this foundation with gold, silver, precious stones, wood, hay, or straw, the work of each will come to light, for the Day will disclose it. It will be revealed with fire, and the fire [itself] will test the quality of each one's work. If the work stands that someone built upon the foundation, that person will receive a wage. But if someone's work is burned up, that one will suffer loss; the person will be saved, but only as through fire. Do you not know that you are the temple of God, and that the Spirit of God dwells in you? If anyone destroys God's temple, God will destroy that person; for the temple of God, which you are, is holy.

—1 COR 3:10–17

In the pale—white room, I wait for Your response.
Fog clings to the floor, if there is a floor,
trying to decide whether to
lift itself from its silent crawl.

You enter in an instant and love me.
Your voiceless command opens the door.
One piercing point of light, darkness—
the vastness of the distance overwhelms me.
Light, my destiny, breeds joy.
Resistance on the threshold is futile.
The allure of promise, of hope, of redemption
intoxicates me.

Fire stings,
dry heat from the desert fills my lungs
in purifying respiration.

Surrendered and clinging to the reins
of Your black smoke chariot,
I am propelled to the light.

Cleansed by the fire, I see it was I who was invited,
when I invited You.

October 25, 2012

"I, the firey life of divine wisdom, I ignite the beauty of the plains,
I sparkle the waters, I burn in the sun, and the moon, and the stars.
With wisdom I order all rightly. Above all, I determine truth."

—HILDEGARD OF BINGEN[1]

On this perfect day, I live Your Wisdom,
entering my soul through my hungry eyes
and devouring the cobalt—blue sky.

Your Wisdom enters my soul through my happy eyes
as I drink in the vision of sparkling water
nestled in its mountain bed.

Your Wisdom enters my soul through my grateful ears
sopping up the laughter from young and old
who play in the water like fish.

Your Wisdom enters my soul through my mouth
sharing a meal sprung from our common home.

Your Wisdom enters my soul through my skin
with the last few drops of soft, golden sunlight caressing my face.

1. Fox, Christian Mystics, day 25

Your Wisdom enters my soul through my heart,
welcoming the stranger into our prayer circle as the shadows grow
longer.

Your Wisdom enters my soul through my entire awareness,
savoring the graces of this perfect day.

October 26, 2012

For the grace of God has appeared, saving all and training us to re-
ject godless ways and worldly desires and to live temperately, justly,
and devoutly in this age, as we await the blessed hope, the appear-
ance of the glory of the great God and of our savior Jesus Christ,
who gave himself for us to deliver us from all lawlessness and to
cleanse for himself a people as his own, eager to do what is good.

—Titus 2:11–14

Brilliant in its gown of white marble,
the amphitheater awaits the community gathering.
All is white, glowing with radiance
not of my world.

Immersed in Your waters, I see You.
Your ruddy face and great eyes
invite me deeper.
Rising from the water,
I climb into Your embrace,
and am dry before I reach You.

Your tangible embrace soothes
and calms me.
You turn me toward the staircase.
My hand in Yours,
as we ascend the staircase.
The higher I climb with You,
the more I diminish into You.

October 30, 2012

So submit yourselves to God. Resist the devil, and he will flee
from you. Draw near to God, and he will draw near to you.
Cleanse your hands, you sinners, and purify your hearts, you
of two minds. Begin to lament, to mourn, to weep. Let your
laughter be turned into mourning and your joy into dejection.
Humble yourselves before the Lord and he will exalt you.

—Jas 4:7–10

"You still resist too much."
Your words startle me because I know You're right.
Being cajoled into that conclusion is part of the problem.

You drop Yourself in among us
who only know fire and food.
How can we know You?

For a moment, we marvel at Your presence . . .
Frightened by what we don't understand,
we press in on You.
Seeing we're not ready,
You flee.

December 11, 2012

"Love is an adventure and a conquest. It survives and develops like the universe itself only by perpetual discovery"
—TEILHARD DE CHARDIN[1]

Tunnel vision confines mother and baby
battling the madness of everyday life.
Relentless chaos attacks from all sides,
prying hope from the mother's heart.

Screams pealing,
baby wrenched from mother's arms
to nestle in arms of the Mother
who can calm the skies.

No chance to love together.
No chance to calm the chaos.
No chance to live and grow together.
No chance for happy endings.

New Mother knows best.
New Mother knows a greater peace.
New Mother knows a greater joy.

1. Fox, Christian Mystics, day 230

Old Mother's tears,
here and now,
flow unabated.

December 14, 2012

Just being still and silent during Eucharistic
adoration as my launching pad.

In Your Narthex majestic bright white walls,
black walnut pillars and crossbeams
glow with promises of future permanence and comfort.

Hand in hand, You pull me close.
But for my resistance, we would be one.
My sadness from disappointing You
competes with Your joy,
mercy,
love,
and life—giving embrace,
to take possession of my heart.

In the center, I rest on the black walnut bench.
Your parting gaze tells me there's more work to do.
Swimming in Your focused regard,
until the entire scene dries up,
crackles, and blows away with the wind—
and leaves me immersed in the sun—scorched desert.

New wind drives a sandstorm,
pelting my being with ferocity,
blasting away attachments
that sully my otherwise pure self.

I stand alone in the solitude of the desert's heat,
remnants of the rage
scrape every element of earthly desire away.
Forward, I trudge, sun searing my torn and raw body.

As I wander, my weary flesh crawls to the crest of a dune.
Clinging to my last ounce of strength,
I peer over the edge and see
Your palace in all its splendor!

January 16, 2013

I urge you, brothers, in the name of our Lord Jesus Christ, that
all of you agree in what you say, and that there be no divisions
among you, but that you be united in the same mind and in
the same purpose. For it has been reported to me about you,
my brothers, by Chloe's people, there are rivalries among you. I
mean that each of you is saying, "I belong to Paul," or "I belong to
Apollos," or "I belong to Cephas," or "I belong to Christ." Is Christ
divided? Was Paul crucified for you? Or were you baptized in
the name of Paul? I give thanks [to God] that I baptized none of
you except Crispus and Gaius, so that no one can say you were
baptized in my name. (I baptized the household of Stephanas
also; beyond that I do not know whether I baptized anyone
else.) For Christ did not send me to baptize but to preach the
gospel, and not with the wisdom of human eloquence, so that
the cross of Christ might not be emptied of its meaning.

—1 Cor 1:10–17

Parents argue over trivialities
fresh from the source of the message,
so fresh from remembering
what he said and why he said it.

Yet they still quibble,
remembering differently,
blindly fighting to the death
to be right.

Is it their humanity that blinds them?
Is their ego so tightly invested in their own ideas
that they see nothing else?
Is their pride refusing to concede to the Truth?

Must they remember differently?
Are they convinced the rewritten history is true?
Even so, the battle comforts me.
It rages today
from its foundation
rooted in Adam and Eve,
where my attachments rest.

January 28, 2013

After he had spoken, a Pharisee invited him to dine at his home. He entered and reclined at table to eat. The Pharisee was amazed to see that he did not observe the prescribed washing before the meal. The Lord said to him, "Oh you Pharisees! Although you cleanse the outside of the cup and the dish, inside you are filled with plunder and evil. You fools! Did not the maker of the outside also make the inside? But as to what is within, give alms, and behold, everything will be clean for you. Woe to you Pharisees! You pay tithes of mint and of rue and of every garden herb, but you pay no attention to judgment and to love for God. These you should have done, without overlooking the others. Woe to you Pharisees! You love the seat of honor in synagogues and greetings in marketplaces. Woe to you! You are like unseen graves over which people unknowingly walk."

—LUKE 11:37–44

Newly ordained takes his seat at the altar,
the sheep believe he can do no wrong.

The women sit under their chapel veils, sweating,
anxious it may be out of place.
Is it long enough?
Is it white enough?
Does it cover my head enough
to prove my reverence to God?

Men, stoic in their pews, wonder how soon this will end,
and their box for salvation can be checked.

Oh, newly ordained, where is your crook?
Without it, what will you use to guide us?

We know why our sins are wrong.
We know why our sins separate us from God.
We need your crook to lead us to intimacy,
a gentle nudge in the right direction when we stray.

Did the Bishop teach you about balance,
fairness, justice?
Did the Bishop teach you about Wisdom?
How Wisdom cannot be possessed—
that we can only allow it to pass through us?

February 7, 2013

(reprise)

"In the interior life there should be moments of relaxation, freedom and 'browsing.' Perhaps the best way to do this is in the midst of nature, but also in literature. Perhaps also a certain amount of art is necessary, and music . . . You also need a good garden, and you need access to the woods, or to the sea. Get out in those hills and really be in the midst of nature a little bit! That is not the only legitimate, it is in a certain way necessary . . . The woods and nature should be part of your solitude, and if it's not periodically part of your solitude I think the law should be changed."

—THOMAS MERTON[1]

We sit in this late winter wood.
The foul decay of winter's loss
gives way to fresh smells of
new life emerging.
The promise of spring caresses my cheeks.

We sit and exist together.

1. Fox, Christian Mystics, day 301

Overtaken by the urge to explore, we hike
The wondrous work of Your creative power,
of water and wind,
of time and patience,
of love and loving,
draws me into the winding gorge.

Stairs carved from the rock elevate us,
cool stone surprises and delights.
Atop the arch, we absorb it all.

And You delight in my delight.

Now to the mountain where we ski.
Frigid air bites my skin—
a reminder I am alive, part of creation!

The beach,
where the hot sun kisses my skin,
bestowing vitamin D through my body.
I am grateful for the blanket,
protecting us from the roughness of the sand.
We swim, and I notice Your wounds.
And wonder why the salty water does not sting You.

"Why do You still have the wounds?"

"To testify of your redemption."

Ending our day of play, we bicycle up the long, steep hill.
We end exhausted, affirming our productive day.

"Why are You playing with me?"

"Because I am human, and I love to play, too!"

February 26, 2013

"Although I have spoken here only of seven Mansions yet in
each there are comprised many more, both above and below
and around, with lovely gardens and fountains and things so
delectable that you will want to lose yourselves in praise of
the great God Who created it in His image and likeness."

—Teresa of Avila[1]

My courtyard teems with fountains and gardens
lush and vibrant with new life.
Glowing subtly, pink translucence,
emanating from its depth,
fed from the source,
invites integration with the light.

Behind me, Your hands steady my shoulders.
Your embrace comforts me,
infuses my being with peace.

You lift me to see castles emerging,
spreading vastly, connected to my own.
Higher still, hundreds of thousands more.
Connected higher still, each, too numerous to count,
forms a glowing orb, pulsing with life.

1. Fox, Christian Mystics, Day 171

Each glows,
connects to another,
connected to the center,
drawing and giving energy
where the source lives.

March 15, 2013

In the stony outskirts of the city
I saw you scurrying about
a dog pawing through garbage
even children choose a plastic car
over you.

—DOROTHEE SOELLE[1]

Nomadic in this parched land
I search for You,
seeking nourishment.

You
on the horizon,
walking toward me!
Meeting in the middle—
we walk together in silence.

At the place You have prepared for me
our camp is set
with charcoal fire,
blue and red hot,
the centerpiece.

1. Fox, Christian Mystics, Day 266

You cook for me.

Tearing fish from the skewer, You feed me.
I eat and am nourished.

You take the cup, bless it, and pass it to me.
We drink, and my thirst is quenched.

For now.

We sleep.
We wake.
We continue.

March 19, 2013

Now in regard to the matters about which you wrote: "It is a good thing for a man not to touch a woman," but because of cases of immorality every man should have his own wife, and every woman her own husband. The husband should fulfill his duty toward his wife, and likewise the wife toward her husband. A wife does not have authority over her own body, but rather her husband, and similarly a husband does not have authority over his own body, but rather his wife. Do not deprive each other, except perhaps by mutual consent for a time, to be free for prayer, but then return to one another, so that Satan may not tempt you through your lack of self—control. This I say by way of concession, however, not as a command. Indeed, I wish everyone to be as I am, but each has a particular gift from God, one of one kind and one of another.

—1 Cor 7:1–7

Roustabout notices me and draws near,
pretending to be You,
fooling me in his joke.
Dark, imposing form invites itself
into my personal space,
asking for a walk on this day,
in this morning,
heavy with dampness and biting air.

Confused and searching, I stroll beside the false force,
who senses my tension and
reveals itself by deploying its hood,
thinking it to be an act of disguise.

Awakened, I see through the mask and flee,
grateful for sharp senses
toying with meditation
in the controlled environment of my imagination.

March 20, 2013

"Christ in the parable of the sower long ago told us that 'The seed is the word of God.' We often think this applies only to the word of the Gospel as formally preached in churches on Sundays (if indeed it is preached in churches anymore!). But every expression of the will of God is in some sense a 'word' of God and therefore a 'seed' of new life."[1]

In this holy darkness where we meet,
I ask, "What is the word of God?"

Jesus reveals majestic mountain landscapes,
deep river gorges,
ornate church buildings,
a homeless man sitting against a skyscraper,
the Plum Street Temple.

Jesus reveals, "Creation is God's word.
You must protect it.
You must sit and savor God's word all around you."

1. Merton, New Seeds of Contemplation, 14

March 21, 2013

"It is not we who choose to awaken ourselves,
but God Who chooses to awaken us."[1]

You are generous with Your touch
and invite me to be generous with mine.
Your invitation intoxicates.
Your peace fills my being.

Emerged from our holy darkness
to overflowing light and creation,
You show me Your face,
Your transfigured body.
I stroke Your beard,
massage Your shoulders and back,
and probe Your wounds.

Reclining on a blanket in the grass,
breaking bread with You,
the provider of everything.
I provide only myself,
my longing for touch,
my desire to be fed.

1. Merton, New Seeds of Contemplation, 10

March 26, 2013

"One of the most striking examples of loss of natural perception is in the generations of women whose mothers broke the tradition of teaching, preparing, and welcoming their daughters into the most basic and physical aspect of being women, menstruation. In our culture, but also in many others, the Devil changed the message so that first blood and all subsequent cycles of blood became surrounded with humiliation rather than wonder. This caused millions of young women to lose their inheritance of the miraculous body and instead to fear that they were dying, diseased, or being punished by God." [1]

—CLARISSA PINKOLA ESTES

Your transfigured presence pierces
a pinhole of light
through the dark horizon.

Drawing nearer to me, You whisper,
"How you treat your body reflects the
depth of our relationship."

You complete Your journey.
Draw entirely to me.
Your body still shines
but deprives our space of its radiance.

1. Fox, Christian Mystics, Day 290

Why?

The answer to my question is revealed in my asking.
Light fills our space and envelopes me.
In my doubt and insecurity,
I wonder why
nothing but the light fills this space.

"All you need is the Light."

"Will I ever be satisfied?"
"Will I ever realize that's not the right question to ask?"

April 8, 2013

As they approached the village to which they were going, he gave
the impression that he was going on farther. But they urged him,
"Stay with us, for it is nearly evening and the day is almost over."
So he went in to stay with them. And it happened that, while he
was with them at table, he took bread, said the blessing, broke it,
and gave it to them. With that their eyes were opened and they
recognized him, but he vanished from their sight. Then they said
to each other, "Were not our hearts burning [within us] while
he spoke to us on the way and opened the scriptures to us?"

—Luke 24:28–32

"How often do You walk with me
cloaked by my oblivion?"

"I am always with you.
Especially when you meet
the suffering, the imprisoned,
the discarded,
the dispensable.

Your heart knows it.

Your heart wants to yell it from the mountains.

Though your brain desires ignorance
and fears the transformation
that gives you eyes to truly see Me
in the breaking of the bread.
I don't want to vanish in that breaking.
Until your heart
overtakes your brain,
such sight would overwhelm
your senses and repel you."

April 10, 2013

"If you succeed in emptying your mind of every thought and
every desire, you may indeed withdraw into the center of yourself
and concentrate everything within you upon the imaginary
point where your life springs out of God: yet you will not really
find God. No natural exercise can bring you into vital contact
with Him. Unless he utters Himself in you, speaks His own name
in the center of your soul, you will no more know Him than a
stone knows the ground upon which it rests in its inertia".[1]

"Jesus, we walk a lot."
"Yes, we do."
Led forward,
dressed in white.

We sit.

He pours and drinks above the table
covered in pall—like linen.
He extends the cup
with an invitation for me to drink.

"Am I to drink from the same cup?"

1. Merton, New Seeds of Contemplation, 39

His silence overpowers me.
With His loving gaze, continuous,
He passes the cup to me,
and I drink.

May 9, 2013

On this day, I learned our dear friend
received a terminal cancer diagnosis.

"The root of Christian love is not the will to
love, but the faith that one is loved."[1]

I grieve for myself and my wife.
I grieve with you, God whispered.

I rejoice in the strength of our relationship through You.
I rejoice with you.

I grieve for her husband.
I grieve with you.

I rejoice in my friendship with him.
I rejoice with you.

I grieve for the loss he faces.
I grieve with you.

I rejoice in the opportunity to walk with him in his grief.
I rejoice with you.

1. Merton, New Seeds of Contemplation, 75

I grieve for the uncertainty he faces.
I grieve with you.

I rejoice that You will walk with him.
I rejoice with you.

I grieve for her children.
I grieve with you.

I rejoice in the opportunity to grieve with them.
I rejoice with you.

I grieve the loss of all the memories we had yet to create.
I grieve with you.

I rejoice in the memories we have made.
I rejoice with you.

June 19, 2013

"Notice all the things silence does other than be quiet. Silence is real enough to be afraid of. But when integrated into an environment and a way of living, it calms and gradually integrates us into it." [1]

The lovely sound of silence,
full of music from birdsong.
Full of breezes gently lifting
the short, sparse
hairs on my head.

Silence,
full of breezes softly urging
the hair on my arms to lie
in wait against my skin.

Silence,
full of breezes
kissing my cheek
with a reminder of my lover's embrace.
Gentle, soft, full of life.

1. Laird, A Sunlit Absence, 47

Silence,
the trees embrace me,
proving they are Your love.
Proving they are the living word,
professing Your promise of life.

"Who am I to receive such a gift?"
The trees answer:
"A beloved child of God."

Can I bear the silence necessary
to believe it?

July 1, 2013

Ever since the creation of the world, his invisible attributes of
eternal power and divinity have been able to be understood
and perceived in what he has made. As a result, they have no
excuse; for although they knew God they did not accord him
glory as God or give him thanks. Instead, they became vain
in their reasoning, and their senseless minds were darkened.
While claiming to be wise, they became fools and exchanged
the glory of the immortal God for the likeness of an image of
mortal man or of birds or of four—legged animals or of snakes.

—Rom 1:20–23

Lamp, chain, and pendulum
swing from Your hand,
glowing brighter with every oscillation.

Afoot in the desert, we carry on,
deeper into the darkness.
Lamp and chain slicing
through the curtain to
show us the way.

On the precipice,
we gaze on Your people
below
pouring out of their homes
to see who we are.

Individual hearts
contain depth, convolution,
confusion, sadness, and pain—
such simplistic, black and white
language cannot soothe.

"I want you to be My light on a hill
for all to see,
leading each person to know Me
on their terms.

Be an example of love,
mercy, and forgiveness
for all who seek it."

July 8, 2013

"If I were not so mad with my own vanity and selfishness and petty
cares for the ease of my flesh and my pride, I would see clearly
how perhaps nothing I have ever done of any good was mine
or through me but given by God through the love and gifts and
prayers of people who have given me their whole life in fruit for
me to pick and take or spoil according to my indifferent and cursed
selfishness. That fruit has only nourished me in grace in spite of
myself, so to speak, and accidentally given me a little health."[1]

Dawn breaks in Appalachia.
Clarity of sky suggests
the abundance of rain,
thundering down the creek,
is a mirage.

My gratitude runs heavy, deep, and fast,
united with the churning trough of
freshwater cascading from the
mountain.

1. Hart, Montaldo, The Intimate Merton, 21–22

My furry tick—laden neighbor,
my prayer companion,
nudges my hand with his snout
to remind me he's
part of creation, too.

Together, we let the soothing sound—
water crashing on rock—
lull us into our prayer.

Gratitude overflows from
my bond to this little dog,
Shiloh.
His ticks, this land,
and all those around me in
their pre—dawn slumber.

July 17, 2013

". . . how can I write for the poor? How can I tell them poverty
was the condition of Christ and the Blessed Mother on earth and
suffering was Christ's portion when, although I do not make any
money ($45 a month and room and board), the life I lead here
is as happy as the richest kind of life and is comfortable?"[1]

The sickly child struggles to taste
a shared cup of honey
hoisted feebly.

Deep sorrow and suffering
reflected in the stream
that missed his mouth.

Pain compounded,
for lack of nourishment
haunts my heart.
A pang of desire to soothe
the child's despair.
Anguish sparks.
My desire to taste the honey You offer
is strong,
but I long more to help this boy
and his family
receive it and be fed.

1. Hart, Montaldo, The Intimate Merton, 36

July 26, 2013

"Easter is like what it will be entering eternity when you suddenly, peacefully, clearly recognize all your mistakes as well as all that you did well: everything falls into place."[1]

With its savory aroma,
masking the bitter taste,
my coffee draws me in.

The stillness in my cup
agitates,
fills with a vortex of darkness,
enticing me deeper for a ride.

Recognizing the agitation for what it is,
I push against the vacuum,
thirsting to pull me
into its misery.

Refreshed from the struggle,
I lie in interstitial space.
From above, light and clouds tangle in a milky mix,
inviting me to surrender,
to give in.
I oblige the call
with hope, anticipation, excitement.

1. Hart, Montaldo, The Intimate Merton, 54

At the far end,
we dance upon the Milky Way.
The cosmos spreads before us
with the beauty of Your order and creation,
proclaiming
Your goodness and Your justice.

And Your friendship.

Beauty, creation, goodness, excitement,
now tempered by pain, suffering, worry, despair,
and love of a woman younger than she looks,
who gathers her children with vain effort,
while burning seasoned oak wood
smoke lifts and swirls,
remind me again
of Your presence in all things.

August 5, 2013

Standing in a watchtower on The Great
Wall of China as my launching pad.

A sea of umbrellas
in the hot August sun
reminds me I am a foreigner,
welcomed, embraced, wanted,
at least for a while.

Struggle between gravity and grade tires
and weakens my senses
until I reach
the watchtower.

I see your brick, whoever you are.
I touch.
I feel.
My fingers linger to hear your message
in our small connectedness
across millennia.

Under what oppression
did you break your body
to do the will of your king?
Did your survival depend on submitting
your will to your king's will?

Am I exploiting your sacrifice?

October 7, 2013

"The things I thought were so important because of the effort I put into them—have turned out to be of small value. And the things I never thought about, the things I was never able either to measure or to expect, were the things that mattered."

"Between the silence of God and the silence of my own soul stands the silence of the souls entrusted to me."

"The most substantial things are ready to crumble or tear apart and blow away."

". . . the living things sing terribly that only the present is eternal and that all things having a past and a future are doomed to pass away".[1]

Agitated and restless, I arrive, dripping in darkness, searching for You.
Shadowed figures in the distance, faintly visible, gyrate to their own music.

1. Hart, Montaldo, The Intimate Merton, 93–96

The figures advance,
revealing hideous faces, scars, fangs,
and a wicked thirst for my destruction.
Red, fiery eyes pierce my thin skin.
Images increasingly unbearable—
ghastly figures closing in on me . . .

"Save me, Jesus!" I scream.

Burning light pierces the horizon,
dispels the darkness,
sending me running from the answer
to my prayer.

My oblivion comes to awareness to ask,
"Why are we running away?"
Stopping in my tracks,
I face the answer to my prayer.
Light and energy infuse my entire being,
disintegrating all that wants to
destroy me.

October 10, 2013

"...I do not wait for an answer, because I have begun
to realize You never answer when I expect".[1]

The Pascal candle stands in darkness.
Strands of translucent ribbon glow—
dip and sway
in a spiral dance of joy.
An invitation to look more closely.

Intensifying, my gaze transforms
candle and ribbon to a tall, slender flame rising,
fueled by black granules of incense.

Peace permeates my soul,
longing for deeper . . .
Deeper what?
Deeper I know not what,
save the desire to know that depth,
to find life in that depth,
to know that fire,
to find life in that fire.

1. Hart, Montaldo, The Intimate Merton, 98

October 17, 2013

Once when Jesus was praying alone, with only the disciples near him, he asked them, "Who do the crowds say that I am?" They answered, "John the Baptist; but others, Elijah; and still others, that one of the ancient prophets has arisen." He said to them, "But who do you say that I am?" Peter answered, "The Messiah of God."

He sternly ordered and commanded them not to tell anyone, saying, "The Son of Man must undergo great suffering, and be rejected by the elders, chief priests, and scribes, and be killed, and on the third day be raised."

Then he said to them all, "If any want to become my followers, let them deny themselves and take up their cross daily and follow me. For those who want to save their life will lose it, and those who lose their life for my sake will save it. What does it profit them if they gain the whole world, but lose or forfeit themselves? Those who are ashamed of me and of my words, of them the Son of Man will be ashamed when he comes in his glory and the glory of the Father and of the holy angels. But truly I tell you, there are some standing here who will not taste death before they see the kingdom of God."

—Luke 9:18–27

Who do I say You are?
Incessant blathering in an angst—laden rant
spews from my mind.

Ambiguous thoughts of love, life, salvation,
and what You accomplish through me,
babble like a brook from my consciousness
until my heart convinces my brain
I do not have, and will not have
the right words to answer Your question.

Settling me with Your gaze,
You slip in words of wisdom,
melting my anxiety,
setting my heart ablaze in my chest.

"Love is a choice. Choose me, and I will do the rest."

"What does it mean to deny myself?
Giving my spare change to the man asking for it?
Giving food to the homeless person on the corner?
Placing others' needs ahead of mine?
Thinking of myself less and acting from that decision?
Letting the car into traffic when others won't?"

"It's all of that and more."

"And this cross You want me to pick up?
Is it the minor and major sacrifices of comforts
so others can have enough?
Or the added stress associated with increased patience?
Or stopping to help the stranded fix the flat tire?"

"It's all of that and more."

November 4, 2013

He was praying in a certain place, and when he had finished, one
of his disciples said to him, "Lord, teach us to pray just as John
taught his disciples." He said to them, "When you pray, say:
Father, hallowed be your name,
your kingdom come.
Give us each day our daily bread
and forgive us our sins
for we ourselves forgive everyone in debt to us,
and do not subject us to the final test."
—LUKE 11:1–4

Waiting, watching,
basking in your own immersion,
patience waits with us.

Slowly, patience cedes to the allure of agitation,
not yet like you,
and not yet ready to be like you.

Your stillness is so profound,
silence so deep,
Your lack of movement moves us.
We yearn to understand how to touch,
how to feel Your depth.

In our collective consternation,
the bold one asks the question
our hearts cannot contain.

Participation in Your answer burns
a bit of my attachment to myself away.
Not enough to sustain me.

I see through Your simple answer;
You see through my skepticism.

In a fit of agitation and boldness
greater than the first, I exclaim,
"What You are doing is more than You're telling!"

Reply comes with swiftness and sharpness
as truth is wont to do.
"What I have told you is the threshold.
Enter, and you will be enlightened."

November 5, 2013

"In the penitential psalms Christ recognizes my poverty in
His Poverty. Merely to see myself in the psalm is a begin-
ning of being healed. For I see myself through His grace. His
grace is working; therefore I am on my way to being healed.
O the need of that Healing! I walk from region to region
of my soul, and discover that I am a bombed city."[1]

The bombed—out shell of my mansion
lies trapped in the vacuum
of lifelessness,
of hopelessness,
where a billion points of light
offer only mockery and taunting
of the life I seek.

The One billionth—and one point glows
with greater subtlety and nuance
hoping to catch my eye,
and in the catching,
seems more surprised than me.

In my surrender to our connectedness,
my soul and its mansion drift toward that
subtle point.

1. Hart, Montaldo, The Intimate Merton, 113

Escalating intrigue hastens my desire,
my trajectory toward the light.
Renewed speed invites the hint of
warmth.

Hastened desire feeds hastened speed,
heat intensifies, cauterizing brokenness,
germinating the hope of new life yearning
to take a breath from the cleansing fire.

Freedom from the shackles of attachment
to myself reveals my reconstituted castle,
new stone upon new stone, all ablaze with
translucent effusion.

November 7, 2013

And he said to them, "Suppose one of you has a friend to whom
he goes at midnight and says, 'Friend, lend me three loaves
of bread, for a friend of mine has arrived at my house from a
journey and I have nothing to offer him,' and he says in reply
from within, 'Do not bother me; the door has already been
locked and my children and I are already in bed. I cannot get
up to give you anything.' I tell you, if he does not get up to give
him the loaves because of their friendship, he will get up to
give him whatever he needs because of his persistence."

—Luke 11:5–8

In the empty vastness of my soul,
we walk.
In this depth, every part of me You touch
erupts with the vastness of creation.

We climb the mountain
You created in me—
deeper,
higher—
exposing demons when I stray from You on this path.
Apart from You,
I see violence and death.
Close to You, I see beauty and grace.

At the summit, darkness begins,
though I can easily see
the expanse of earth and sea
spread out before me.
Sun creeps below the horizon,
leaving its dramatic gift of
red, orange, and yellow!
Cobalt and crystal—clear ebony
follow closely behind!

"What, at last, does this time with You
have to do with perseverance in prayer?"
You answer with Your loving gaze.
Coolness and loving darkness settle in,
powerless against the fire You've built.

Basking in the warm glow of the burning,
we enjoy each other's company
with my question answered
in this enjoyment.

November 14, 2013

"...Our life is a powerful Pentecost in which the Holy Spirit, ever active in us, seeks to reach through our inspired hands and tongues into the very heart of the material world created to be spiritualized through the work of the Church, the Mystical Body of the Incarnate Word of God."[1]

Mountain, alone,
snowcapped and majestic,
far on the horizon yet fills my vision.
I resign myself to its seduction,
navigate the foothills laying in its shadow.
Dawn breaks with expected silence,
shedding itself of the burden
carried from the other side of the world.

My pace toward the base
mirrors the sun's as it groans upward,
halting momentarily.
The moon eclipses its trajectory,
casting more shadow in the valleys.

1. Hart, Montaldo, The Intimate Merton, 116

Grateful for the brevity
of the blackout
and ensuing sharpened vision,
my eyes bathe in the image—
thousands of golden pixies
climbing the cliffs and waterfalls
etched in the prominence.

All of them at once
beckon me hasten to join them,
through waves of thousands of tiny hands.

Accepting the invitation,
I'm there in a flash,
dressed in gold,
scaling the mountainside,
climbing the waterfalls.
We fly as one bird,
up, down, around, and through,
seeking unity with each other
and the mountain.

November 20, 2013

As he continued his journey to Jerusalem, he traveled through
Samaria and Galilee. As he was entering a village, ten lepers met
[him]. They stood at a distance from him and raised their voice,
saying, "Jesus, Master! Have pity on us!" And when he saw them,
he said, "Go show yourselves to the priests." As they were going
they were cleansed. And one of them, realizing he had been healed,
returned, glorifying God in a loud voice; and he fell at the feet of
Jesus and thanked him. He was a Samaritan. Jesus said in reply,
"Ten were cleansed, were they not? Where are the other nine? Has
none but this foreigner returned to give thanks to God?" Then
he said to him, "Stand up and go; your faith has saved you."

—Luke 17:11–19

You approach our fringe society.
The sight of You
unites us in You and the world
for a heartbeat.

Hearts burning,
we run to meet You—
stopped short by the law.

In our last and only hope,
we cry out to You
for blessing and healing
which flows from Your heart,
free and abundant.

On our way to the authority,
we see and feel our healing.
Joy blooms from my heart
and the hope of spring
courses through my veins.

I urge my companions to turn back with me.
We, in our healing—our new vision and perfection—
can embrace Him now!

They refuse, persisting in their embrace of divisiveness.
Eagerness to return to their former way of life consumes them.
Their severance stings.

How could anyone return to a former way of life,
after experiencing such depth
of love
of healing?

I turn in my solitude,
running to Him.
His gratitude and love
overflow my infinite soul.

November 21, 2013

Where then do I stand? Have I the courage to stand on my own feet,
or do I have feet to stand on? What has it meant to stand on them?[1]

In the dark of night,
the moon ignites the pristine sky.
The sky touches infinity
while the stone well house stands, ominous,
daring me to enter.

I stare deep into the abyss.
The well of evil oozes,
satisfied it has made its
presence known.

Hearing my cry for help,
the full moon stretches—
sweeps me from this wretched place
to the safety of her bosom.

Gazing from the dark side
into Your vastness
I see You glowing red and pink.
All of creation connects to You.

1. Hart, Montaldo, The Intimate Merton, 119

I dive into You,
swim in You,
through You,
with You,
with the multitudes.

Through that portal moon
I gaze back,
aware of the wreckage
the evil has wrought.

A man sleeps in the cold.
Women and men creep down the highway
to participate in the grind.
The weight of their drudgery, their despair,
stifles and stupefies.

At Your nudge,
I beckon them to the light
and delight in their joyful "Yes!"
"Go get more."
"Who shall I get?"
"Many."

November 24, 2013

Feast of Christ the King. From a reading
proclaimed during Mass.

> ...giving thanks to the Father, who has made you fit to share in
> the inheritance of the holy ones in light. He delivered us from
> the power of darkness and transferred us to the kingdom of his
> beloved Son, in whom we have redemption, the forgiveness of sins.

—COL 1:12–14

Ashore on the inland sea,
nestled in the mountains,
mist mingles with sun
to veil the vastness.
I see You.

As You walk away,
the surf dances around Your ankles.
"Why walk away from me?" I ask.
"Why turn away from me?"

"I'm not walking away from you," You say.
I'm inviting you to follow Me!"

December 11, 2013

> He gives power to the faint,
>   abundant strength to the weak.
> Though young men faint and grow weary,
>   and youths stagger and fall,
> They that hope in the Lord will renew their strength,
>   they will soar on eagles' wings;
> They will run and not grow weary,
>   walk and not grow faint.

—Isa 40:29–31

Come to me, all you who labor and are burdened, and I will give you rest. Take my yoke upon you and learn from me, for I am meek and humble of heart; and you will find rest for yourselves. For my yoke is easy, and my burden light.

—Matt 11:28–30

As if outside of myself
I see You set Your yoke upon my shoulders.
It is light!
It is easy!
It fits well!

From inside of myself,
I see You behind me
and feel much of the weight is in Your hands.

I see You in me from years gone by,
when children would help me
clean out the rubble of a useless past.
Eager to help, they grabbed
the boulders, the garbage bags,
the piled junk we foolishly collected
for tomorrow.

They lift and heave,
not knowing the burden is on me.
Grateful, I leave my dream,
aware You carry the load,
delighting in my effort to help.
Just as I delight in the children's
efforts to help me.

December 16, 2013

When he had come into the temple area, the chief priests and
the elders of the people approached him as he was teaching and
said, "By what authority are you doing these things? And who
gave you this authority?" Jesus said to them in reply, "I shall ask
you one question, and if you answer it for me, then I shall tell you
by what authority I do these things. Where was John's baptism
from? Was it of heavenly or of human origin?" They discussed
this among themselves and said, "If we say 'Of heavenly origin,'
he will say to us, 'Then why did you not believe him?' But if we
say, 'Of human origin,' we fear the crowd, for they all regard John
as a prophet." So they said to Jesus in reply, "We do not know."

—MATT 21:23–27

Your hand wraps around mine,
leading us into play.
Down the slide, up the ladder,
the rhythm repeats,
manifesting our joy at play.

The gift of Your mountain
rising boldly from Your green, grassy plain.
Our running, skipping, cartwheeling
continues to delight us.

"What does Your story about authority
have to do with Advent?"

"The story is not about authority.
The story is about honesty and
confidence in what you believe.

Concerned about political and cultural ramifications
of their answer,
the Elders were blinded from the truth
and could not answer,
nor witness to it.

Honesty in your belief
helps bring forth the reign of God,
what Advent is about."

February 8, 2014

"Jesus could only speak from the experience of life. To be attuned to him and share his experience of God, one had to love life and plunge into it, open up to the world, and listen to the creation."[1]

You saw Your daily bread
sown in a field—
harvested,
ground into meal,
infiltrated by yeast,
kneaded.

Your connection to creation
speaks to us today.
Food for our bodies,
sun to warm us,
shade to cool us,
sweet air to tickle our noses,
autumn colors to bring glory to our eyes.

Let that creation touch
the fabric of my soul.
Bring me understanding.
How can we dance with creation,
flourish in it,
give it new life?

1. Pagola, Jesus, An Historical Approximation, 58

February 13, 2014

"Kairos! Everything for a long time has been slowly leading up to this and—with this reading—a sudden convergence of roads, tendencies, lights, in unity! A new door. (I looked at it without comprehension nine months ago)."[1]

Planted atop the snow—laden mountain peak,
I bask in the clarity of sky, wind, and mind.
Wind pierces my skin—
proves to my doubting soul
I am alive!

Clinging to the top of the world
Your creation lays before me.
Whisper and wind invite me to surrender
to the carpet of juts, jags, and river valleys
etching their way to seas
far from here.

1. Hart, Montaldo, The Intimate Merton, 167

You come to this place
inside me.
Sit with me in silence.
We consume every precipice,
every cap of snow,
every ponderosa pine,
every river
following Your finger
digging slowly into the earth.

"I made this for you."

Heart burning, I leap with joy,
overflowing with gratitude.
Not over the gift given,
but over Your knowledge of who I am,
Your knowledge of what draws
me closer to You.

February 19, 2014

"It is a peculiar problem of our time when we come from a world that is completely opposed to our ideal and do not really 'come from it' but only bring it along with us."[1]

Alone on that ridge, hovering over my soul,
drawn to that familiar fire,
deeper in the place I long to be,
You bid me, "Come!"

I see the beauty of Your glow,
Your welcoming invitation.
Fire rises high against the rock wall,
now maneuvered a bit further inward.

"Jesus, who am I?"

"You are a gift of talent and skills.
The love meant to connect others to Me.
You are the joy infusing
those you encounter.
Treat all others with love and respect,
because they are like you, too.
All are different in skills and talents, but
very much like you in mission and purpose."

1. Hart, Montaldo, The Intimate Merton, 172

"Your glow! What is it?"

"My glow is your essence.
The brighter My glow,
the more in tune with Me you are."

February 20, 2014

"Father I beg you to teach me to be a man of peace and to help bring peace to the world. To study here truth and non-violence and patience and the courage to suffer for truth."[1]

Lonely,
I walk in isolation in a familiar forest,
encased by trees
thick with life,
occluding my view of the light.

The clearing ahead
reveals the tension
between dim light and canopy—
each struggling to dominate,
neither strong enough to prevail.

In that place of struggle, ivy invades.
Blanketed by the heavy air,
I find rest between light and dark.

Struggling to escape this gray area,
I seek the snowy peak,
where sun flows freely,
air is light.
You meet me in my futility.

1. Hart, Montaldo, The Intimate Merton, 174

"Trust me," You implore.
"You need to be here just a
little while. Let me lead you."

"Yes. Lead me."

March 3, 2014

"It is absurd to inquire after my function in the world, or whether
I have one, as long as I am not first of all alive and awake."[1]

The fiery dawn reveals Your presence
on the monk's hillside
as Your body harnesses
the breaking of light across the horizon.

Feet planted firmly on the earth,
You stand majestically over Your creation.
The breeze from Your waving arm
jostles the birds, who rise from the trees
to greet You on this new day.

Awaking eagerly, they lift themselves to Your call.
In formation,
they circle You in a tight spiral,
happy to lose themselves,
happy to be united in flight and song,
filling the morning,
giving glory to Your presence.

1. Hart, Montaldo, The Intimate Merton, 176

April 24, 2014

Now a week later his disciples were again inside and Thomas was
with them. Jesus came, although the doors were locked, and stood
in their midst and said, "Peace be with you." Then he said to Thomas,
"Put your finger here and see my hands, and bring your hand
and put it into my side, and do not be unbelieving, but believe."
Thomas answered and said to him, "My Lord and my God!" Jesus
said to him, "Have you come to believe because you have seen
me? Blessed are those who have not seen and have believed."

—JOHN 20:26–39

How much You must love me and desire my love
to offer such probing I would only allow a clinician!

How do I respond to an offer
I could never make myself?

How do I return Your overture of intimacy
when I'm not willing to let You probe and heal my wounds?

Heal me, Jesus, so I can be willing to surrender enough
to let You explore my brokenness
and heal me where only You know I hurt.

May 6, 2014

"... now is the time I must learn to stop taking satisfaction in
what I have done, or bring depressed because the night will
come and my work will come to an end. Now is the time to
give what I have to others and not reflect on it. I wish I had
learned the knack of it, of giving without question or care."[1]

In the evening's blue hour,
I step onto the bricked patio—
grass and pebbles littering
the space between.
Dim porch light permits
a glimpse of the beauty and love
ahead of me,
dressed in olive skin and
a provocative red gown.

Her glance beckons me to stroll with her
along the creek
where darkness and water mingle
to form unintelligible muttering.

1. Hart, Montaldo, The Intimate Merton, 197

She gazes deeply into my eyes,
and I am intoxicated by
a wave of eros, philos, agape,
and every other kind of love
we don't have names for.

Approaching a dark and deep pit, I ask,
"What's down there?"

"Do not look down there.
You are not ready.
Others, prepared, have seen.
But not you, not yet."

With a wave of her slender arm,
lights ablaze the hillsides
cradling me.
The lights are more brilliant,
more vibrant,
more colorful,
more pleasing to the eye,
more everything.
Magis!

"What I am showing you
is the new heaven and earth
I have created for you."

Rounding the bend as we walk,
Behold! The orb glowing in the sky!
Shining without blinding,
revealing the secret—
the hills have no source of light of their own,
but reflect the light of the source.

"How do I give without reflecting on it?
How do I learn the knack of it?"

"Don't try to create a situation,
to be a witness.
Be a witness first.
Allow true creativity
to spring forth from your spirit."

May 10, 2014

"Sunrise—an event that calls forth solemn music in the very depth of one's being, as if one's whole being had to attune itself to the cosmos and praise God for a new day, praise Him in the name of all the beings that ever were or ever will be . . ."[1]

Fresh on top of this hill, I sit.
Fire crackles next to me,
a reminder of the chill
inches from my insulation.

Darkness—
broken by the slim crack of brilliant orange,
red colors reflect the blaze—
knows continued resistance is futile.

In this emergence of light,
I sit in my soul with awe and wonder.
And gratitude.
You planted Your law of love in our hearts,
calling us to bathe in this light,
calling us to let the gentle fire
from afar
kiss our eyes and cheeks.

1. Hart, Montaldo, The Intimate Merton, 202

I leave with a sense of knowing
the other side of the world better,
having shared the source of life
and love
and energy
that conceives growth and connectedness.

June 5, 2014

"... (Desegregation can be brought about by any-
one, but integration only by the Holy Spirit")[1]

Quiet, resting at our spot in the woods,
blue jeans and flannel
humanize You in Your divinity.
Whether it was an hour or a day
I do not know.
What I do know—
Your peace fills me,
overflowing into my outer self.

Rising, walking, climbing higher,
I follow until Your creation
spreads out before me,
reflecting the lush, vibrant essence of Yourself.
As far as I can see, life abounds
full to the brim.

The creator hovers,
emanating familiar and familial red—pink glow
that speaks to us of love
and warmth
and safety.

1. Hart, Montaldo, The Intimate Merton, 226

Reaching the highest point of the ridge,
multitudes of humanity emerge,
radiating, glowing,
from Your lush, vibrant essence
to saturate my vision with life.

With song on their lips,
multitudes sing
to the glory of the creator,
fueling the great wind
rushing, swirling, infusing
all being with life,
driving more song, more wind, more life!

Never tiring,
the great wind pulls the creator toward us,
hurtling increasingly faster,
more lovingly,
more giving,
crashing, smashing, integrating
itself into creation,
infusing this new earth with new life.

Bibliography

John of the Cross, *Ascent of Mount Carmel*. Translated by E. Allison Peers. 2008. Radford, VA. Wilder.

Eldredge, John. *Beautiful Outlaw: Experiencing The Playful, disruptive, extravagant Personality of Jesus*. New York. Faith Words, 2011.

Fox, Matthew. *Christian Mystics: 365 Readings and Meditations*. Novato. New World Library.

Teresa of Avila. *Interior Castle*. Translated and edited by E. Allison Peers. 1961. Reprint. New York, Image Books, Double Day 2008

Hart, Patrick, and Montaldo, Jonathan, eds. *The Intimate Merton: His Life from His Journals*. New York. Harper One. 1996

Pagola, Jose A. *Jesus: An Historical Approximation*. Translated by Margaret Wilde. Miami: Convivium, 2012.

Merton, Thomas. *New Seeds of Contemplation*. New York. New Directions, 2007.

Laird, Martin, OSA. *A Sunlit Absence: Silence, Awareness, and Contemplation*. Oxford: Oxford University Press, 2011.

CPSIA information can be obtained
at www.ICGtesting.com
Printed in the USA
LVHW020010111121
702983LV00013B/1356